EGYPTIAN MYTHS

Retold by Jacqueline Morley

Illustrated by Giovanni Caselli

HODDER
Wayland

First published in Great Britain in 1999
by Macdonald Young Books

Reprinted in 2001 by Hodder Wayland,
an imprint of Hodder Children's Books

Hodder Children's Books,
A division of Hodder Headline Ltd
338 Euston Road
London NW1 3BH

Editor: Lisa Edwards
Designer: Dalia Hartman

A CIP catalogue for this book is available from the
British Library.

Printed and bound in Portugal by Edições ASA

ISBN 0 7500 2608 1

CONTENTS

INTRODUCTION

The stories in this book, although very old, are probably new to you. Perhaps you have heard of the Ancient Greek and Roman gods – Venus and her son Cupid, Jupiter the thunderer, Mercury with winged sandals and so on. They have never been forgotten. The gods of Ancient Egypt, no less marvellous, are less well known because Egyptian myths ceased to be remembered and retold. Instead, they became entombed in a dead, indecipherable language.

The temple inscriptions and sacred texts that described the Egyptian gods were written in hieroglyphs, a form of alphabet in pictures. During Ancient Egypt's immensely long history – over three thousand years – writing became simpler, until finally only the temple priests understood the complicated old inscriptions. As Egyptian civilization crumbled, the stories were gradually forgotten. In the 6th century AD, the Christians closed the last temples; soon nobody remained who knew the old gods. It was not until after 1822, when the Frenchman Jean Champollion managed to decipher hieroglyphs, that the tales of the powerful and magical beings who appear in this book were rediscovered.

The images of these gods appear strange, with their heads of birds and beasts. Their gaze, terrifyingly severe, reflects the awe in which they were held. For the Egyptians had reason to feel themselves at the mercy of their gods. Apart from a narrow strip along the banks of the River Nile, their land was entirely desert. Their lives depended on this fertile ribbon of land watered by the annual flooding of the river. The flood seemed like a miracle to them – a gift from the gods. Unless they received continual praise and offerings the gods might no longer send the flood. Only the Egyptian kings, the all-powerful pharaohs, could ensure that they continued to do so. The

people believed each pharaoh was a god on earth and that when he died he would rejoin his father the Sun God, and obtain his blessing for the land of Egypt.

There were a host of Ancient Egyptian gods and goddesses. Each region had its local gods, and at various times over the centuries different ones enjoyed particular fame. When the early pharaohs ruled from Memphis, Ptah, god of that city, was worshipped as creator; later he was outshone by Ra of Heliopolis. When the capital moved to Thebes, the Theban god Amun became supreme. The Egyptians, believing that different gods could in some mysterious way be one, renamed him Amun-ra.

There must have been a wealth of stories about these gods. On surviving wall decorations we can still read the gods' names and see what they looked like, but in too many cases the myths that belonged to them have been lost. We must be thankful for those that have survived. Much of what we know of creation and the afterlife comes from prayers and spells carved or painted in tombs. The earliest surviving examples to be found, in the pyramid at Saqqara, are 4,300 years old. Other vivid details of the afterlife have been preserved through the later custom of burying with the dead a papyrus (the Ancient Egyptian equivalent of a book, written on a long roll of paper made from the papyrus reed) containing essential instructions for a safe journey to the next world. Sometimes inscriptions tell a tale: the myth of Horus comes in part from the walls of his temple at Edfu; the story of the Lord of the Nile was inscribed on a rock in upper Egypt. A number of legends and magical tales survive in writings on papyrus, although part of the papyrus is often missing – which is why the story of 'The Three Crowns' ends rather abruptly. In the case of 'The Doomed Prince' more has disappeared. The Egyptologist George Ebers supplied an ending based on similar folk traditions, and I have taken my cue from him. See if you can tell where the papyrus breaks off and guesswork begins. The answer is on page 63.

JACQUELINE MORLEY

RA THE SHINING ONE

In the beginning, before the world was made, there existed one thing only, a vast ocean called Nu. What its waters contained is a mystery. If there were powers hidden in its depths, those powers had no names, and for the Ancient Egyptians a thing that had no name could not exist.

Then a voice said from the waters, 'I am Ra, the Shining One.' Immediately the great god Ra appeared, the All-powerful One, who created himself by speaking his own name. He had many names, all of which he spoke at the beginning of time. All, that is, except his most sacred and powerful name and that he kept secret and did not speak.

'My name is Khepri at dawn, Ra at noonday and Tum in the evening,' he declared. Immediately he became the sun that is born in the east, blazes in the midday sky and fades rosily into the west. And so the first day was made.

Whatever Ra imagined in his heart and named with his mouth – behold, it existed! So by the power of his thoughts he brought the world into being. He said, 'Shu,' and Shu the Air was created. He said, 'Tefnut,' and Tefnut the Rainmaker filled the air with moisture. He called forth Geb the Earth, and his sister Nut the Sky, the children of Shu and Tefnut. He named the gods of the earth and the sky and all the things in the seas and on dry land. He named the River Nile that watered the land, and the land he named Egypt.

Ra looked on the land with his fiery eye – the Eye of Day which is the sun – and the Eye shed burning tears. As the tears touched the earth they became living people, the first men and women in the world. 'I will teach the people I have made how to live,' said Ra. So he took on the shape of a man and ruled Egypt as its first pharaoh and his reign lasted many thousands of years.

At last, however, Ra grew old, for while he lived on earth he felt the passing of time. Then some of his subjects began to speak scornfully of him, 'Ra is old,' they said. 'His bones have become silver, his flesh is gold and his hair is like lapis lazuli. He can no longer rule us. We need a new leader.' And they plotted with Apophis, the Serpent of Evil, to overthrow Ra.

Ra saw the wickedness in the hearts of his people and was angry. He summoned all the gods to his council chamber – Shu and Tefnut and Geb and Nut and all the other gods he had called into being. Even watery Nu came from the depths to bow down before him. When all were assembled, Ra spoke, 'Hear and know that rebellion has been plotted against me, so that I long to destroy people utterly. Tell me, is it not fitting that I should turn my Eye on them and scorch them?'

Then all the gods trembled at the fury of Ra. Only Nu was brave enough to speak, 'Ra, Lord of All Things, your throne is steadfast and cannot be shaken. Many fear you and will not follow Apophis the serpent,

so do not, we pray you, let your Eye burn up the land of Egypt entirely. Seek only those that are rebellious and tear them to pieces.'

Ra replied, 'I will send my Eye into the world as Sekhmet, to destroy the guilty.' Then Sekhmet, a terrible lioness, leapt from the Eye of Ra. Thirsting for blood, she bounded into the desert hills where the conspirators had hidden themselves. She swiftly scented them out, killing and destroying and rejoicing in her work, until she waded in blood. All day she hunted and ate and at night she slept. But by the next morning her throat was dry and needed more blood. Up and down the land she prowled, tearing people limb from limb, the good and the bad. No one could stop her. And day by day her hunger grew, until the Nile ran red with blood.

Ra saw that Sekhmet was beyond control and must be tamed. He called swift messengers and told them, 'Run with the speed of shadows to the island of Elephantine that lies below the first cataract of the Nile and bring me the red ochre that is found there.' The same night the messengers returned, bearing baskets full of the red earth. Then, by Ra's command, the priestesses of the Temple of Ra crushed barley and steeped it in red ochre to make beer as red as blood.

By dawn, seven thousand jars of beer had been emptied before Sekhmet's lair, flooding the land to a depth of three hands. When Sekhmet awoke and saw the red flood she laughed and licked her lips and drank greedily, for she thought it was more blood. She drank until she could drink no more and fell into a deep and drunken sleep. She did not stir till evening came, so that in all the day she did no harm to any living thing.

Then Ra summoned her. 'Return to me in peace,' he called, and Sekhmet came to him and gently hung her head. 'Fair and gracious daughter, I will give you a new name,' said Ra. 'No longer are you Sekhmet the Slayer. Your name is Hathor the Comforter of Humankind. Rule my people, not through fear but through love.'

So the great mother-goddess Hathor, Queen of Love, was born and the people of Egypt were freed from terror. Ever afterwards, in memory of that day, a festival of Hathor was held at the New Year, marked by great celebrations and the drinking of vast quantities of intoxicating beer.

THE BIRTH OF OSIRIS

When the world was new, Geb the Earth and Nut the Sky lay together in a close embrace, for they loved one another dearly and would not be separated. When Ra saw that the beautiful goddess Nut loved Geb much more than she loved him he was filled with jealous anger. He ordered Shu the Air to come between the lovers and keep them apart. At Ra's command Shu raised Nut's body above his head on outstretched arms and kept her there, so that the sky arched high over the earth. Nut could now only gaze down longingly at Geb, since she could touch him only with her feet, which still rested on the eastern horizon, and with her fingertips, which she

The Birth of Osiris

stretched down towards him in the west. Nevertheless, it was not long after this that Thoth, the ibis-headed God of Wisdom, came to Ra with news that greatly displeased him. 'Nut, the Lady of the Skies, is expecting a child,' he said, 'and if she gives birth to a son he will one day replace you as ruler of Egypt.'

Now Thoth was Lord of All Knowledge, both human and divine; he was master of all the arts and sciences and it was he who taught the people of the earth the art of writing and the use of numbers. He invented hieroglyphs and plotted the courses of the stars in the sky. He was a great magician who could foresee the future. So Ra was angry and troubled when he heard Thoth's words, for he knew they would come to pass unless a way could be found around them. 'No child of Nut shall take my throne from me,' he cried, 'for Nut shall never have a child! I, who created time and divided the years, and numbered the days of the year to be three hundred and sixty, now curse Nut with this curse – that she shall not be able to give birth in any hour of any day in any year. Neither in this year nor in any

❖ 11

year to come!' Ra was triumphant, for he imagined that in his cleverness he had found a way to defeat Thoth's prophecy. Even though its words might be true, their truth could not matter.

Nut heard Ra's words and wept bitterly. Her grief was so great that all the gods felt sorry for her, but they knew that the words of Ra could never be unsaid. Thoth was especially moved by her tears, for he loved Nut and it was his prophecy that had caused her sorrow. He told her not to lose all hope, for he had a scheme in mind that would defeat Ra's curse.

Thoth went to his friend Khons the moon god and suggested that they should while away the night in playing draughts. Khons was very ready for a game. 'But the loser pays a forfeit,' Thoth added. 'Very well – agreed!' said Khons. So they settled down to play, and Thoth won the first game easily.

'What do I have to pay you?' asked Khons.

'Just a little of your moonlight', Thoth replied.

Khons smiled at this, for he had plenty of moonlight to spare; he paid

the forfeit and demanded another game, for he was determined to beat Thoth sooner or later. They played a second game, then another and another. The result was always the same, for Thoth was a player that nobody could beat. Khons was forced to part with more and more moonlight; his beams grew weaker and weaker until they could hardly light the night at all. And from the time of that unlucky draughts game, the moon has not been able to shine as brightly every night as it used to. It has to hoard its light carefully, and some nights are very dark; the moon shows its full face only once a month.

Thoth had won so much light that when he added it all together there was enough to make five whole days. He slipped these days in between the end of the old year and the beginning of the new, so that they were not part of either year. During these five extra days, Nut's five children were born: first her sons, Osiris on the first day, Haroeris upon the second, and Set upon the third; then her daughters, Isis upon the fourth day and Nephthys upon the fifth.

Ra was furious to discover that he had been outwitted. He was too late to prevent it, but he declared that in future he would claim these five days as his own and fit them into his years, which then would have three hundred and sixty-five days each – just as they do today.

The birth of Nut's eldest son, Osiris, was marked by a great marvel. A voice spoke, from whence no one knew, saying, 'The Lord of All is born.' And in the course of time this came to pass, for Osiris became first the King of the Living and then the King of the Dead. How this happened, the next four stories will tell. In the meantime, Nut entrusted her firstborn to Thoth, who brought him up in secret away from the anger of Ra.

THE SECRET NAME OF RA

Ra, Lord of the Gods, was filled with anger when the five children of Nut the sky goddess were born, for it had been foretold that one of them, Osiris, was destined to rule Egypt in his place. Ra did his best to stop them being born, but the cunning of Thoth, the God of Wisdom, outwitted him. But as time passed and Nut's children grew up, Ra overcame his anger and welcomed them to his Council Chamber, to join the company of the gods. For he still continued to rule in Egypt as pharaoh, although he had grown by now very old indeed.

Osiris, the first-born son of Nut, married Isis, her first-born daughter, and their marriage was a happy one. Osiris was kind and just, for he had been taught by the wise god Thoth, and put his lessons to good use. Isis had been Thoth's pupil too, but the lessons she had liked most were those that dealt with magic. She had begged Thoth to teach her the secrets of his magic powers, but of all his knowledge this was the only part that he was wary of revealing. However, Isis was so clever and eager to learn that he let himself be persuaded against his better judgement. He taught her the spells that give mastery over spirits, and those that cure diseases and revive the dead. He also shared with her the Secret of Secrets – the power of names. Before long, Isis became a great enchantress and worker of spells, as skilled a magician as her teacher.

The prophecy made about Osiris was not forgotten; almost all the gods agreed that none looked more like a future king than he. But such talk filled Isis with impatience. She wanted Osiris to be king now, and she wanted to be queen and first among the goddesses, in heaven and on earth. So she decided to force Ra to give up the throne to Osiris. The wisdom of Thoth had taught her that only by learning Ra's most sacred secret name could she

gain power over him. But she knew she could never persuade Ra to tell her the name – she would have to force it from him. She consulted her books of magic, made her plans and cast her spells.

Ra was now so aged that as he sat in majesty on his throne he sometimes nodded asleep; his head lolled forward and spittle dribbled from his mouth. Isis watched, and collected Ra's saliva from the ground where it fell. She mixed the saliva with earth and modelled this clay into a serpent with poisoned fangs. Then she placed this magic serpent on the path that Ra would tread as he walked through the land of Egypt, which he did daily to see that all was well with his creation.

At the usual time, the god arose and went on his way, with his attendants, and when he passed the serpent it shot out its tongue and bit him. It was a bite like fire, consuming his body so that he cried out in agony; his teeth chattered, his lips trembled and he became speechless. His cries brought his attendants running. When his powers of speech returned he told them he had been bitten by some unknown creature that was not of his making. He commanded them to summon every god known to be skilled in magic, to see if any of them knew a charm to drive this poison out and free him from his torment.

Isis was summoned with the others. 'What has happened, divine Father?' she asked. Ra told her that he was smitten by an unknown evil that his Eye had not seen, nor his hand made. He felt hotter than fire and colder than water and his sight was fading. Then Isis said to him cunningly, 'Father, tell me your name, for he who utters his hidden name shall live.'

Ra answered, 'My name is Maker of Heaven and Earth; my name is Binder Together of the Mountains; my name is Creator of the Waters, Stretcher of the Two Horizons, Maker of the Gods. I open my eyes and there is light; I close my eyes and there is darkness. I make the hours, I create the days; I open the year, I send the Nile flood, I make the breath of life. My name is Khepri in the morning, Ra at noon and Tum in the evening.' But while he spoke the poison bit deeper into him until he could no longer stand.

Then Isis said to him, 'O Father, among all the things you have named to me, you have not named your hidden name. Tell me that name and the poison will come forth.'

In his extreme agony, Ra agreed to tell Isis his name. He did not speak

it, but it passed from his heart to her heart, so that it remained hidden from the rest of creation.

Isis, with the secret name of Ra now in her heart, then spoke this spell, 'Flow poison, from the flesh of Ra. I am the worker of this wonder. I overcome the serpent and spill its venom upon the ground. Let it come forth at the command of Isis, she who alone knows the Lord of Creation by his true name.'

So Ra was made whole again. After this he gave up his worldly kingdom and withdrew to rule the heavens, where he was immortal and never grew old. He was seen no more on earth, and Osiris became Pharaoh of Egypt.

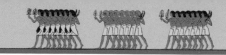

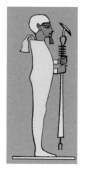

THE TREACHERY OF SET

When Ra, the first ruler of this world, retired to heaven, Osiris, the just and gentle son of Nut the sky goddess, became Pharaoh of Egypt. He found its people living like animals, or worse than animals. Their lives were unguided by any laws; they did not even know how to grow food. They ate only flesh and existed by hunting with spears and slings. If they failed to kill any wild thing they turned on each other and ate their own kind – which animals do not. Instead of living in settled towns and villages, they wandered in disorderly tribes up and down the land, always restless and continually fighting and killing each other. Osiris showed them how to live civilized lives. He made wise laws, and encouraged his people to obey them and live peaceably together. He taught them to praise the gods and to build magnificent temples in their honour. He gave men and women instructions on how to farm the land, so that it yielded plentiful crops of wheat and barley, and how to grow fruit trees and to cultivate the grapes for wine. Soon peace and prosperity replaced anger and want, and the people of Egypt loudly praised Osiris the Good.

But not all the gods were pleased. Set, the brother of Osiris, hated him for his success. Set was the god of storm clouds, thunder, and the cruel hot desert. In the desert dwelled evil things – scorpions and wicked spirits, drought, whirlwinds and sandstorms; these were the servants of Set and came when he called them to do his bidding. Set mocked the good works of Osiris, secretly waiting for an opportunity to get rid of him.

When it seemed to Osiris that all was going well with his kingdom, he entrusted it to Isis, his beloved queen, while he went on a long visit to foreign lands. He wanted to spread to other peoples the blessings that he had

showered on Egypt, so instead of taking soldiers and weapons of war he took priests and musicians, carrying his message of wisdom and peace in music and song. He was everywhere welcomed, and courteously heard.

Meanwhile, Set thought his chance to snatch the kingdom of Egypt had come. Deceitfully, he offered to lift some of the heavy burden of government from Isis's shoulders. But she refused, not trusting him for a moment, and watched his every move. Set worked cunningly to outwit her. He began to speak secretly in people's ears and, as one can always find mean-spirited people who envy success, he managed to gather together a band of seventy-two conspirators to join him in a plot.

When Osiris came home at last in triumph, Set announced a celebration in his honour. There was to be a feast, and Set let it be known that everybody would receive rich presents. The feast ended and the gifts were given out to great rejoicing. Then Set declared that there was one more present still to come. His servants carried in a splendid chest made of ivory and ebony inlaid with silver, and set it in the middle of the room.

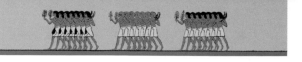

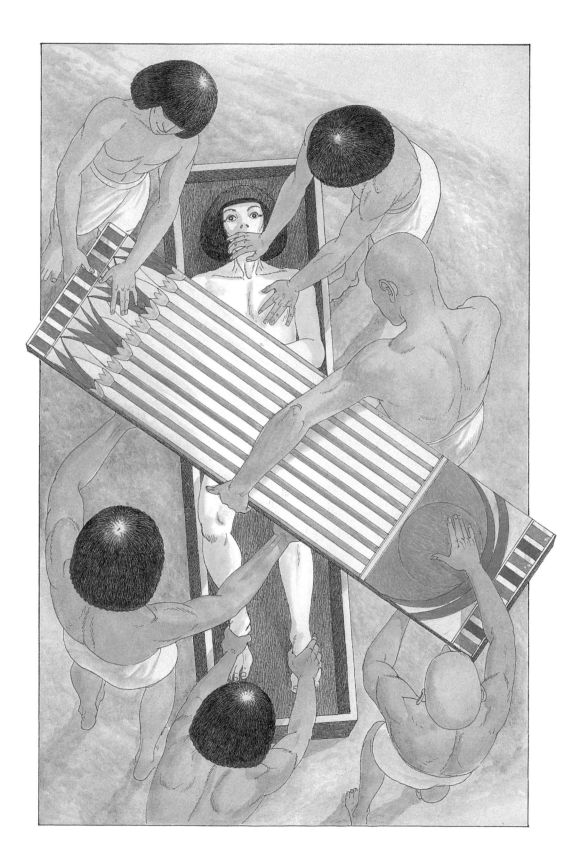

The courtiers crowded around. 'Who is to have it?' they asked.

'That is for you to discover,' replied Set. 'It is a gift to the one who fits it best'.

Then there came a scramble as the guests tried one after another to see if they could fit into the chest, but for some it was too long and for others too short, for some too narrow and for others much too wide.

'And you, brother Osiris, why do you not try?' asked Set.

To please his brother, Osiris lay down in the chest and it fitted him exactly – as Set had made sure it would.

Immediately the seventy-two conspirators surrounded the chest. They rammed down the lid and nailed it fast. They poured molten lead into every crack to make sure that no air could enter. Then they took the chest that had become Osiris's coffin and secretly flung it into the Nile.

The terrified guests ran through the palace telling the news of the murder, while the flood waters of the Nile swept away the chest and bore it down to the sea. The waves of the sea tossed it this way and that, bringing it at last to a foreign shore, close to the city of Byblos in Syria. A large wave carried the chest high up on the beach and washed it up to a young tamarisk tree that grew on the shore. The tree sensed that a god had come to rest near it. It clasped the chest tightly in its branches and grew closely round it, until the chest was quite enclosed inside the tamarisk trunk. The tree flourished and grew wonderfully, so that all who saw it were amazed at its size and beauty. The King of Byblos, admiring the delicious scent of its wood, ordered it to be cut down and its trunk made into a pillar to adorn the great hall of his palace. This was done, and everybody marvelled at the great beauty of the pillar, though none dreamed that it held the body of a god.

Meanwhile Set sat on the throne of Osiris and was Pharaoh of Egypt.

THE WANDERINGS OF ISIS

O siris, the wise and just King of Egypt, was murdered by his treacherous brother Set. Why and how is told in another story in this book. There also you can read how the chest which held Osiris's body was carried out to sea and, unknown to anyone, came to be imprisoned in a pillar in the hall of the King of Byblos. Meanwhile, in Egypt, Osiris's loving wife Isis cut off her hair as a sign of mourning and gave herself up to grief.

Her sorrow was the greater because she was about to have a child, which would now have no father to protect it. While Isis was grieving, Set seized his chance. He declared himself Lord of Egypt and imprisoned her in a spinning-house where flax was spun into thread by slaves.

'Spend your time spinning and weaving a shroud,' he told her with an evil laugh.

Isis was comforted in her misery by the wise god Thoth, whose spells undid the locks of her prison. 'Flee far away and hide,' he urged. 'Set will not rest until he has destroyed you too.' So when night came, Isis ran from the house in the darkness, accompanied by seven scorpions sent by Thoth to protect her on the journey. Two followed behind her, two walked on either side and three went ahead to ensure the safety of the path.

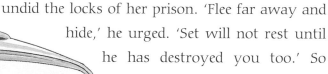

After much journeying, Isis knocked at a house to ask for a night's shelter. The rich woman who lived there slammed the door in her face. This callous behaviour enraged the scorpions and they took a horrible revenge. Six of them added their poison to the tail of the seventh, which crawled under the door and stung the woman's baby with seven-fold poison. The woman shrieked and howled when she found her dying child. Isis, who had been given shelter by a poor fisher girl, was filled with pity for the mother. 'The child shall not die through no fault of his own,' she said, and she commanded the poison to depart. When the rich woman saw her son restored to life she took all her fine possessions and filled the fisher girl's hut with them. This she did in honour of Isis, whom the poor fisher girl had helped when she had not.

Isis found a hiding-place in the swamps of the Delta, where the Nile divides to form many islands; there her son Horus was born, on the island of Chemmis, among the papyrus reeds. Isis entrusted her baby to the care of Wadjet, the kindly snake-goddess of the Delta and set off to search for the body of Osiris, for until he had been given a proper funeral his spirit could not enter the Land of the Dead. But before she left she loosened the island from the river bed and sent it floating on the waters, so that Set should not find it.

For a long time Isis searched in vain. Nobody she questioned knew what had happened to the chest containing Osiris's body. Then one day

some children playing near the river told her they had seen a splendid chest swept by the current towards the open sea. Isis summoned up the demons of the sea to help her. 'If you can make the King of Byblos cut down the finest pillar of his palace, you will have what you seek,' they said, and they told her the fate of the chest.

Isis then unfurled a pair of mighty wings, and flew across the sea to Byblos. The moment her feet touched the shore she shed her god-like form and became an old beggar woman. She sat beside a well, grieving and silent, until the maidservants of the Queen of Byblos came to draw water. These

she greeted humbly and asked to be allowed to plait their hair. Into each plait she breathed a delicious perfume, so that when the women returned to the palace their mistress, Queen Astarte, demanded to know how their hair came to smell so sweet. When she heard of the woman by the well, the queen had her brought to the palace and liked her so much that she made her nurse to her baby son.

The baby boy, who had been thin and weakly, flourished so amazingly under Isis's care that the queen, who at first had been delighted, grew suspicious. She feared that the stranger was using magic arts and began to watch her closely. Knowing that Isis nursed the child by the fire in the great hall when everyone else was asleep, the queen hid and watched. She saw Isis lay the child in the flames. Then, while the fire played over him, she transformed herself into a swallow and flew round and round the pillar,

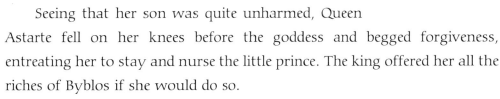

uttering sad cries. The horrified queen dashed forward and snatched her son from the flames. 'Foolish mother!' exclaimed Isis, appearing before the queen in all the brightness of a god. 'Had you not interfered I could have made your son a god, as I am. The fire was burning away all that was human in him. But now he will be no more god-like than any other child.'

Seeing that her son was quite unharmed, Queen Astarte fell on her knees before the goddess and begged forgiveness, entreating her to stay and nurse the little prince. The king offered her all the riches of Byblos if she would do so.

'I cannot stay,' said Isis, 'nor do I need your riches. But I will leave your child my blessing in return for one thing. Give me whatever you shall find within the pillar of this hall.'

The king at once gave orders for the pillar to be split apart and the chest containing her husband's coffin was discovered within. Isis flung herself upon it and shed bitter tears. Then she wrapped the rest of the pillar in fine linen, anointed it with scented oil and gave it to the king and queen, who placed it in the temple at Byblos. This temple became a place of pilgrimage, as people flocked to worship the wood that had held the body of a god.

Isis brought the coffin secretly to Egypt by boat and hid it in the marshes while she returned to her baby, Horus. But on that very night, Set and his followers came boar hunting in the marshes, by the light of the full moon. As Set splashed through the reeds he came upon the hidden chest and recognized it. He broke it open and tore the body of Osiris into fourteen pieces which he scattered throughout the length of Egypt.

Then weary Isis began her search once more. She made a boat of

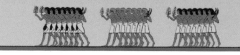

papyrus reeds in which she travelled up and down the Nile looking for the pieces of Osiris's body. She was helped by her sister Nephthys, who though she was the wife of Set had little love for him. They took no rest until they had recovered every piece. They gathered them together and wept loudly over them. Their cries were heard by Ra who sent the jackal-headed god Anubis to them. Anubis showed them how to bind Osiris's body together with linen bandages. This, it is said, was how the first mummy came to be made (for the Ancient Egyptians wrapped their dead in this way). Isis watched over the mummified Osiris and tried to fan life back into his nostrils with her wings. But her magic powers could restore him to a half life only, so that Ra decreed that he should live again to rule in the Duat – the Land of the Dead.

HORUS THE AVENGER

The goddess Isis had every reason to fear her evil brother Set, for he had murdered her husband Osiris and made himself King of Egypt in his place. If Set suspected that she now had a baby son he would not rest until he had destroyed him, for this child, Horus, was the rightful heir. To protect her baby, Isis hid him in the marshes. There she lived as a beggar woman, going out daily to beg for food and leaving Horus tucked away among the papyrus clumps. But Set could not be deceived; his cunning found her secret out. One day Isis returned to find her baby son lifeless. Set had come scuttling in among the reeds in the form of a scorpion and poisoned him. All Isis's magic proved useless; she could not bring him back to life. She seized him in her arms in an agony of grief. Her cries were so terrible that Ra heard them from the height of the sky and halted the Boat of the Sun in which he voyaged daily. The sun stopped and time stood still. Ra sent Thoth down from the heavens to find out what was wrong. Thoth took the child in his arms and spoke these healing words, 'Waken, Horus! Live to rejoice the heart of your mother. Live to destroy the enemy of your father. Live to sit upon the throne of Osiris – Horus the Great Hawk, Horus the Sun Beetle, Horus the Avenger!'

When Isis saw that Horus lived again she begged Thoth to take care of him, so that these words should be fulfilled. So Thoth watched over his upbringing and Horus grew strong and vowed to drive his wicked uncle and all his followers out of Egypt.

When Horus was old enough to claim the throne he put the matter to the Council of Ra. 'I, the son of Osiris, should rightly be king,' he told the assembled gods.

Shu the Air supported him. 'Justice should prevail over strength. The

son should inherit before the mother's brother. Give the throne to Horus.'

And Thoth the All-wise said, 'That is right a million-fold.'

Isis gave a cry of joy and called to the North Wind to carry the news to Osiris. But Ra was displeased that a decision had been made without consulting him. 'Let Set have his say,' he commanded.

So Set spoke. 'I am the strongest of the gods,' he said. 'I dare to do what others fear to do. Would you give the kingdom to a weakling? Would you give it to a mere boy when an older kinsman has a claim?'

Some of the gods were impressed by this, which made Isis lose all patience. She turned on Set in a fury, pouring curses on his head. He swore he would obey no court of which Isis was a member.

Ra then declared that the Council would have to settle the matter later in the day. It would meet upon an island in the river, and he gave orders that Nemti the ferryman should on no account row Isis across in case she caused more trouble.

But Isis disguised herself as an old bent woman. 'Ferry me over the river,' she begged. 'I need to take these barley cakes to my grandson who minds the cattle.'

'I can ferry no woman across,' said Nemti.

'Do I look like Isis? I will pay you a barley cake to take me over.' The ferryman had to agree that she did not look at all like Isis, but a barley cake would not do. He would only ferry her for the gold ring on her finger, which Isis had to give to him.

On the far bank Isis found the gods feasting. Transforming herself into a dazzling young girl she easily attracted the eye of Set who had a weakness for women. When he put his arm around her she burst into sobs and told him she was in great distress. 'My husband was a herdsman, but he is dead and my brother has seized all the cattle that should have gone to my son.'

Set was enslaved by her beauty and rashly exclaimed, 'The son should inherit before the mother's brother! I will defend you.'

'Out of your own mouth you condemn yourself!' cried Isis and she flew over the heads of the gods in the shape of a bird and sang aloud what Set had said.

The gods at once declared the matter was settled – Horus was the rightful king. But Nemti the ferryman had his toes cut off for taking a bribe.

Set was not to be so easily defeated. He summoned an army of wicked followers to fight Horus and all those who had loved Osiris. The battle raged up and down the Nile. Horus soared like a hawk into the eye of the sun, where he became a winged disk which swooped down upon the evil ones. Their eyes could not see and their ears could not hear for the brightness and terror of it. They killed each other in their confusion until all were dead. Yet Set rose again and led a new army of crocodiles against Horus's boats. Then Horus's crew threw chains into the water to entangle the crocodiles, and killed them with spears. But Set, in the form of the hissing Serpent of Evil, escaped into a crack in the ground.

And so the battle was renewed. From the north of Egypt to the south and

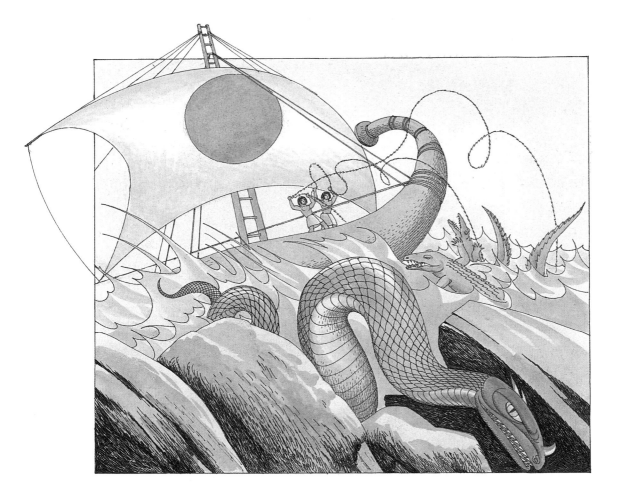

back again, the armies of Set and Horus fought for more than eighty years. Finally Horus challenged Set to a duel to the death. When she learned this, Isis brought her son a glittering boat, ornamented with gold upon the prow.

'In this boat you will be victorious,' she said, 'for you fight for the throne of your father and my spirit is with you.'

Now Set, in the form of a giant red hippopotamus, waited for Horus beyond the city of Edfu. When he saw the golden boat approaching he cursed Horus with a terrible voice that rolled like thunder from the southern heavens to the northern heavens. The people of the earth trembled to hear it. Immediately a

great wind rose, and a raging tempest lashed the waters of the Nile to a fury. Horus's boat was tossed this way and that, but he stood on the golden prow, a towering figure, and held his course unshaken by the storm that beat upon him. A great harpoon was poised in his hand, for Horus had seen the red hippopotamus just below the water, waiting to topple the boat and swallow him. Directly Set raised his nostrils above the surface the mighty harpoon struck his head and sank deep into his brain. Such was the end of Set, the Evil One, the murderer of Osiris and the enemy of Ra.

At once the waters were stilled, the sky grew clear and the people of Edfu came out to welcome Horus, singing praises. 'Let all the dwellers in Egypt rejoice! Horus has destroyed his enemy and the enemy of his father. Eat the flesh of the vanquished, drink his blood, burn his bones in the fire! Let him be cut to pieces and the shreds be given to cats and the entrails to the worms. Praise to Horus the Brave, Horus the Striker, Horus the Avenger!'

Then for many hundreds of years Horus reigned as pharaoh. Yet some say that Set's spirit did not die; that Horus and Set, good and evil, continue their struggle in the world today. But Horus will finally destroy his enemy, and then Osiris and the gods will once more come to earth and all people will dwell in peace.

THE LORD OF THE NILE

Long ago, when the world was new, the gods lived on earth and were pharaohs in Egypt. By their wise example they showed its people how their land should be governed and made them content. The last god to rule on earth was Horus, the son of Isis. When he saw that his people lived peaceably together and had learned to bless the gods, he withdrew to the heavens and let mortals rule in Egypt. The people of Egypt still believed their pharaohs to be gods and thought that each one, when he died, would join his father Ra, and travel with him in the Boat of the Sun. Before departing, each pharaoh built an 'everlasting home' – a tomb in which his body would be preserved forever. For the Ancient Egyptians believed that without an uncorrupted body to live in, the soul would die.

Now, about four thousand six hundred years ago, Zoser, a good and just king, ruled Egypt as pharaoh. He was anxious that his life in the next world should be blessed, but when he looked at the massive brick tombs of former pharaohs he doubted whether even they would last for ever. So he asked his vizier, the great architect Imhotep the Wise, to build him a truly god-like tomb that would outlast time itself. Imhotep created a tomb of stone, which was like many slabs of stone set one upon another, making a stairway to the sky. This was the first pyramid, known as the Step Pyramid, and it still stands today.

In the eighteenth year of Zoser's reign, the story goes, disaster struck Egypt. The Nile, which every year flooded the land, was low and sluggish. Farmers waited anxiously for the river to coat their fields with the rich mud in which the crops grew tall, and to fill the canals that watered them, for rain is hardly known in Egypt. But the flood failed, and when Set sent the burning winds from the desert all growing things shrivelled and died.

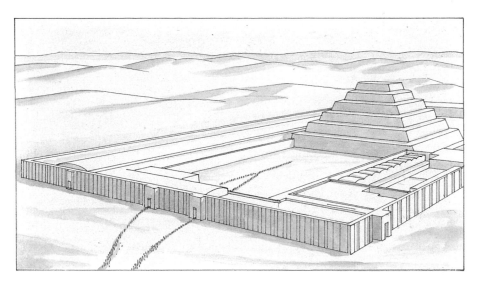

Then Zoser fed his people from the granaries that held the surplus harvests of past years. But for seven years the Nile failed to flood, and then when the granaries were opened they yielded only gusts of empty air. People grew desperate; the strong stole from the weak; the old and the sick were left to starve. Angry crowds beat upon the doors of Zoser's palace demanding he should use his god-like powers to make the river flood.

Zoser was at his wits' end. He had no idea how to make the Nile rise. Then an idea came to him.

'Call Imhotep,' he commanded. 'There is no man living wiser than he.'

Imhotep listened thoughtfully to the pharaoh's agitated questioning, 'Where is the birthplace of the Nile? What god or goddess rules there? I must be told, that I may beg this being to send my country life.'

'Great Pharaoh,' Imhotep replied, 'I do not know, but at the Temple of Thoth at Hermopolis there are sacred books in which these secrets may lie hidden. I will go to Hermopolis, and if Thoth guides me I may learn the truth.'

Before many days had passed Imhotep returned with an answer, 'You must seek the mystery of the Nile in the beginning of all things. In the far south is an island called Abu, which means the City of the Beginning. This was the first dry land to rise from the waters of Nu. Here Ra stood when he spoke the names of all things. Here lies a cave where the river rests each year and is reborn. Then, with new strength it rushes forth through two caverns, which are the breasts that nourish the land of Egypt. The lord of

this cave is Khnemu the Nile god. Only he can make the river flood again.'

Zoser, in his royal barge, sailed southwards up the Nile for many days. At last he came to Abu, the birthplace of the Nile, and entered the Temple of Khnemu, which was a humble wooden building with a door made of reeds and a roof of the branches of trees. Zoser bowed before the shrine and piled offerings on the altar of the Lord of the Nile – bread-cakes, beer, geese, legs of oxen and all the things that please the gods.

Suddenly, in the darkness of the shrine, a majestic figure with the head of a ram with widespread horns appeared before him. This Being addressed him sternly, 'I am Khnemu the Maker who knitted your body together and gave you a heart. I am Nu of the great waters, who was in being at the beginning of time. I am the Lord of the Nile. When I draw back the bolts of the cavern doors and strike the earth with my sandals, the flood pours out upon the land and the people of Egypt are fed and rejoice.'

Then Zoser asked fearfully, 'Lord of the Nile, how has your servant offended you that for seven years you have not sent the flood?'

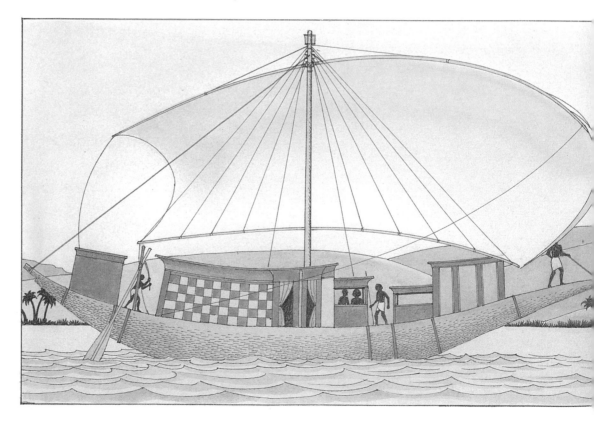

'Why does Pharaoh build for himself an everlasting home of stone, so splendid that the like of it has never been on earth before, and yet neglect the gods?' Khnemu replied. 'My temple stands on banks of granite, which is called the stone of Abu. And here are gold, silver, copper, lapis lazuli, crystal, and alabaster. Should these things lie untouched in the ground, while the Temple of Khnemu is a mere hut of reeds? Restore to the gods the honour that is their due and the Nile will rise again.'

'It shall be done,' said Zoser.

So Imhotep made a temple for Khnemu that outshone all others in the land. Its shrines were filled with statues of gold and silver and its walls were of malachite and lapis lazuli. And the pharaoh decreed that the harvests of the land for many leagues to the north and south of it should belong to the Temple of Khnemu for ever, so that his altars should never be bare. Then once more the Nile watered the land and the fields were yellow with ripe grain. But, from that time on, no pharaoh forgot that the wealth of Egypt, the comfort of its people and the glory of its kings, were the gift of the Lord of the Nile.

THE THREE CROWNS

Pharaoh Khufu, builder of the Great Pyramid at Giza, was a mighty ruler. Yet legend tells of a prophecy that his family would not reign for long, and all Khufu's power could not frustrate it. This is how the story goes:

Khufu was anxious for his pyramid to be perfect within and without, to seem like the work of the gods. Now he had heard that when Thoth, Lord of All Knowledge, taught humankind the art of building, he made a secret record of certain magical designs and calculations which were not for all to know. These records were known as the Plans of the House of Thoth. Somewhere in Egypt these plans were hidden, and Khufu longed to discover them. He questioned the wise men of his court and the priests of the temples of Memphis but they could tell him nothing. Although he enquired of every learned man in his kingdom, not one knew how to find the Plans of the House of Thoth.

One day the pharaoh's son came to him and said, 'O Pharaoh and Father, life, health and strength be to you! I have heard of a magician older and wiser than any other. He is a hundred and ten years old and has the strength of a young man, for he eats five hundred loaves of bread a day, and a haunch of beef, and drinks a hundred jugs of beer. He can reunite a head with its body after they have been severed and restore their life; he can make a lion follow him like a dog. He will surely know the whereabouts of the Plans of Thoth.'

'Where does he live and what is his name?' asked Pharaoh.

'His name is Dedji,' his son replied. 'He lives three days' journey away.'

'Fetch him to me immediately!' Khufu commanded. So the prince sailed up the Nile and found the old man lying in his doorway having his feet and shoulders massaged. He showed no surprise at seeing the prince but

returned his greeting courteously. The prince told him that Pharaoh wished to see him immediately and if he came to the palace he could live there in comfort for the rest of his days. The magician agreed to come, provided that all his children and books might accompany him. Two boatloads of them followed the royal barge that carried him to Memphis.

Pharaoh was waiting for him impatiently. 'Why have I never seen you before?' he asked.

'He does not come who is not invited,' replied the magician. 'When you sent, I came.'

'Is it true that you can restore a head to its body and give it life?' Khufu asked.

'Indeed I can, O Pharaoh.'

Pharaoh turned to his Chief of the Guard. 'Bring a prisoner and cut off his head!' he commanded.

But Dedji said, 'O Pharaoh, why kill a man when a beast would serve?'

So a goose's head was cut off, and the head was put on one side of the hall and the body on the other. Dedji spoke words of power and the head moved towards the body; when they met, the goose stood up and cackled. The same experiment was conducted with a duck and an ox. Both were restored to life. Pharaoh was delighted.

'Tell me, sorcerer of a hundred and ten years,' he said, 'do you know the hiding-place of the Plans of the House of Thoth?'

And Dedji replied, 'A coffer stands in a secret chamber in the Temple of Ra at Heliopolis, and it holds the Plans of Thoth.'

'Then bring me this coffer,' said Khufu.

'O Pharaoh, it is not I who can bring it to you,' answered Dedji.

'Who then?' cried Pharaoh. Dedji answered, 'The eldest of the three sons of Ruddetet shall bring it.'

'Who is this Ruddetet?' demanded Khufu.

Dedji answered, 'She is the wife of a high priest of Ra and she has three sons, still in her womb, who are children of Ra, who has promised her that they shall reign in Egypt.'

Pharaoh's face darkened with anger. 'My son shall sit upon this throne after me, and after him his son!' he said.

'O Pharaoh, health, strength, life be to you!' said Dedji. 'And to your son and your son's son – that they may reign in Egypt before the kingdom passes to the sons of Ruddetet.'

But these words did not soften Pharaoh's anger. He thought no more of the Plans of Thoth, but after brooding for a long time he said, 'I must be informed of the birth of these children, that I may visit them.'

When the day arrived that Ruddetet was to give birth, Ra, the hawk-headed King of the Gods, summoned Isis and her sister Nephthys, and Meskhent the goddess of birth, and the frog-goddess Neket the Midwife, and Khnemu who gives the breath of life, and said to them, 'See that Ruddetet is safely delivered of her children, who are to be kings of Egypt.'

The goddesses disguised themselves as dancing-girls and Khnemu followed them as the porter who carried their props. They knocked on the door of the high priest's house. 'Women,' cried the priest, 'this is no time to dance, for my wife labours in childbirth.'

'We understand these things,' said the goddesses. 'Let us go in to her.' So they went in and shut the door on the priest.

Then Isis brought the first child safely out of its mother's womb and called it User-ref. Meskhent prophesied that he would become King of Egypt

and Khnemu gave him strength. And the second child Isis named Sah-ra, and the third Keku, and Meskhent said, 'These also shall be kings,' and Khnemu gave them strength.

The dancers told the priest that all was well, and he gave them a sack of barley in thanks. Khnemu put it on his shoulder and the gods set off. But as they went along Isis said, 'We should have left some thing of wonder behind, as a token that these are royal children.' So the gods made three golden crowns and hid them in the barley. Then they created a great downpour of rain, very rare in Egypt, and knocked on the door of the priest's house asking to leave the barley in his storeroom to keep it dry, saying they would call for it another day.

Some days later, Ruddetet told her maidservant to fetch barley to make beer. 'There is none left,' said the girl, 'apart from the sack of the dancing girls.'

'Use that,' said her mistress. 'My husband will replace it.'

So the serving maid went down to the storeroom where she heard singing and the sound of instruments playing, and joyful shouts like those that greet a king. Seeing no one, she ran in a fright to her mistress. Ruddetet went to the store, looked in chests and tilted oil jars and turned the storeroom upside-down to find out where the sounds came from. At last she put her ear to the barley sack and heard the singing from within. She opened the sack and saw the crowns. Afraid to touch them, she retied the sack and put it in a sealed chest. When her husband returned, she told him of the signs left by the dancers. 'Ra will favour us,' said he, 'but we must keep his favours secret.'

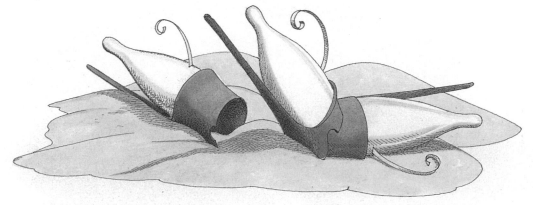

Soon afterwards Ruddetet's maidservant, a slovenly girl, angered her mistress and received a beating. The girl skulked off and planned revenge. 'I will see that Pharaoh hears of this business of the three crowns,' she said. 'He will not leave three kings alive in Egypt.'

She hastened to her eldest brother to get help in carrying her story to Pharaoh. She found him on the floor binding bundles of flax. 'Why come to me?' he asked. 'I shan't help you to tell tales,' and he struck her in the face with a bundle. In a sullen fury the girl went to bathe her smarting face in the river. There Ra sent a crocodile, which snapped its jaws on her and carried her away.

The girl's brother, passing through a courtyard, saw Ruddetet with her head bowed in despair on her knees.

'What troubles you, mistress?' he asked.

'My servant has gone to Pharaoh to betray my children to him,' she replied.

'Your servant will never speak to Pharaoh,' the man told her. 'She went to the river and was eaten by a crocodile.'

Then Ruddetet rejoiced that Ra's will was done, and her children lived on to become pharaohs in Egypt.

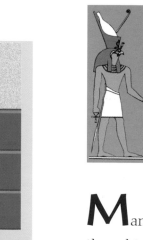

THE BOOK OF THOTH

Many of the wisest men in Ancient Egypt studied magic, for it was thought to be the path to the highest wisdom. Thoth, Lord of Learning, was also the god of magic powers. The book that contained his most secret wisdom, the Book of Thoth, was lost. It was said that whoever found it would possess all knowledge.

Now among the sons of the warrior pharaoh, Ramses II, was a prince named Setna, who spent much time in studying books. One day, in the temple library of Amun-Ra at Thebes, he came across the writings of a prince of long ago called Nefer-ka-Ptah who claimed to have found the Book of Thoth.

On the Book's first page was a spell to enchant all created things, whether in the skies, the earth, the seas, or the mountains, and to understand the language of all beasts and birds and fishes. And on the second page was a spell to see Ra rising in the heavens, and the moon god seated in the moon, and the ocean depths with all the powers that move in them.

Then, added in another hand, Setna saw words that made him tremble – the Book of Thoth had been taken by Nefer-ka-Ptah on his last journey, and laid in his tomb at Memphis.

Setna persuaded his brother Ankh-Herru to search with him for the tomb. They wandered in the ancient royal burial-ground at Memphis, reading the inscriptions, and at last stumbled on the half-buried entrance to Nefer-ka-Ptah's tomb. Setna's brother trembled when they saw the dark shaft leading downwards. 'Stay here if your courage fails,' said Setna, and stepped alone into the tomb.

But the tunnel grew lighter rather than darker. A light shone from the burial chamber where the mummy of Nefer-ka-Ptah lay in an open coffin

of polished granite. On his chest lay a papyrus scroll and it was this that lit the chamber, for this was the Book of Thoth. As Setna stretched his hand towards it a voice, close to him, spoke, 'Return, unhappy man. Do not touch the Book of Thoth, the source of all wretchedness.'

In the shadows sat a woman with a small boy beside her; the cold glimmer of their faces revealed them to be neither the living nor the dead – each was a ka, the spirit double that dwells in each of us (or so the Egyptians thought) and does not forsake us, whether we live or die. 'I am the ka of Ahura, the wife of the prince who lies before you. I watch beside him here for ever, together with the ka of Merab our beloved child. Only thus can we three be together, for Merab and I lie buried far away at Coptos. The Book of Thoth caused our unhappy separation. Listen, and be warned.

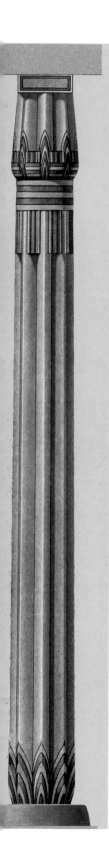

'My husband was a student of magic. I knew nothing but happiness with him until the day he met an aged priest, who, for a hundred bars of silver, sold him the secret of how to find the Book of Thoth. The old man said, "The book you seek lies in an iron box deep within the bed of the Nile at Coptos. Inside the iron box is a bronze box, inside the bronze box is a box of cinnamon wood, inside the box of cinnamon wood is a box of ebony and ivory, inside the ebony and ivory box is a box of silver, inside the silver box is a gold box, and in this lies the Book of Thoth. Scorpions and snakes and every kind of evil reptile guard the iron box, and around it is coiled a serpent that no man can destroy."

'Though I knew that this knowledge was a curse, my husband persuaded his father, the pharaoh, to let him sail to Coptos, and by my tears I made him take me also and Merab our son. A fair wind carried us to Coptos, where we made offerings in the Temple of Isis. Nefer-ka-Ptah then asked the priests for wax, which he made into a boat, with men of wax for its crew. He set the boat on the water and said words of power, and the boat was real and the crew lived. He stepped into the boat saying, "Row, row," and they rowed him out into the Nile, while I stayed on the bank and wept.

'When the boat was over the place of the box, Nefer-ka-Ptah again made an enchantment and the waters divided so that the boat rested on the river bed. He said to the men of wax, "Dig, dig," and they dug deeper and deeper for three days until they reached the iron box and its evil guardians. Nefer-ka-Ptah stilled the snakes and scorpions, but his magic was powerless against the serpent that no man can destroy. As often as he hacked it into pieces with his sword it came together again. Then he thought to put mud on the cuts, and the serpent could no longer reunite itself. So Nefer-ka-Ptah opened the boxes and took out the Book of Thoth.

'On the first page he read the spell to enchant all created things, whether in the skies, the earth, the seas, or the mountains, and to understand the language of all beasts and birds and fishes. And on the second page he read the spell to see Ra rising in the heavens, and the moon god seated in the moon, and the ocean depths with all the powers that move in them.

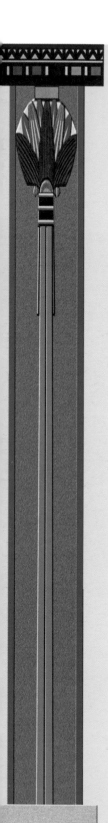

'Then my husband returned to me on the river bank; he put the Book into my hands and I too read the spells. Then Nefer-ka-Ptah copied the spells upon a sheet of papyrus and steeped the papyrus in beer so that the writing was dissolved into it. He drank the beer, so that the knowledge of the spells could never leave him, and we turned the royal boat north and sailed for Memphis.

'But Thoth was full of anger with my husband and complained to Ra, who replied, "He and all that is his are in your power, to do with as you will." Then it was that Merab, leaning from the boat, was drawn into the river and drowned. With bitter tears we put back to Coptos where he was embalmed and entombed. We set sail once more, but at the spot where Merab perished, I too was drawn into the river and drowned. My distraught husband returned to Coptos and laid my embalmed body beside that of our son. Then he turned the boat for the third time towards Memphis; when it reached that city he was discovered dead in his cabin with the Book of Thoth upon his breast.'

Prince Setna listened to this story in fear and awe. Nevertheless he put out his hand to take the Book of Thoth. Then the mummy of Nefer-ka-Ptah reared up in its coffin and demanded a contest for the Book, 'Play draughts with me. If you win, the Book is yours.' Setna agreed, and they began to play. Nefer-ka-Ptah won the first game and uttered a spell that imprisoned Setna in the earth to his ankles; he won the second and Setna sank to his waist. After the third game, Setna sank up to his chin; it was plain that Nefer-ka-Ptah meant the earth to swallow him entirely.

In this desperate strait, Setna shouted to his brother at the entrance, 'Ankh-Herru, run and fetch from the temple sanctuary the Great Amulet of Ptah and set it on my head before I lose another game.'

Ankh-Herru ran like the wind, returning just in time to set the amulet on Setna's head as the mummy played its last move. Setna sprang up, seized the Book of Thoth and fled with his brother.

Nefer-Ka-Ptah said to his wailing wife, 'I will make Setna bring back the Book of Thoth with a goad in his hand and a pot of fire on his head, and he will beg me to take the Book from him.'

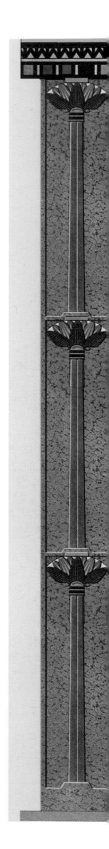

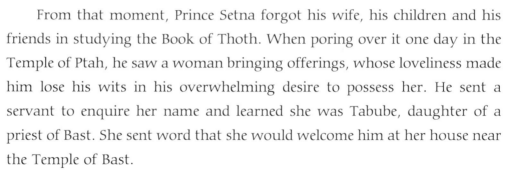

From that moment, Prince Setna forgot his wife, his children and his friends in studying the Book of Thoth. When poring over it one day in the Temple of Ptah, he saw a woman bringing offerings, whose loveliness made him lose his wits in his overwhelming desire to possess her. He sent a servant to enquire her name and learned she was Tabube, daughter of a priest of Bast. She sent word that she would welcome him at her house near the Temple of Bast.

At the appointed hour, Tabube greeted him with smiles and led him to a chamber where a banquet waited. Setna at once declared his undying love for her.

'I will be yours,' she said, 'but I will have no rival. Divorce your wife and give your possessions to me.' Immediately Setna wrote a deed doing all this. 'But your children may dispute this,' said Tabube. Setna's children suddenly appeared beside him and he made them sign away their inheritance. Then Tabube said, 'Your children may plot against me. Let them be killed and cast to the cats of Bast.'

'So be it,' replied Setna. So Setna drank wine with Tabube and while he drank he heard the bodies of his children being ravaged by the cats.

'Now I am yours,' said Tabube and she wrapped her arms around him. But her arms were dry bones; her embrace was cold as death. Setna shrieked and fell, and awoke to find himself lying naked in the street.

Passers-by stared at him, but one stopped to offer him a cloak and ask what afflicted him.

'The madness of Thoth,' Setna replied.

'Go home,' said the stranger, 'and you will find your wife and children safe.'

Setna went home and to his unspeakable joy it was so. 'I will give back the Book that made a sane man mad,' he said, 'and I will carry it back to Nefer-ka-Ptah with a goad in my hand and a pot of fire on my head.'

So Setna returned to the tomb and laid the Book of Thoth upon the dead man's chest. And the mummy rose and spoke, 'Restore to me also my wife and child, Prince Setna. Bring me their bodies from Coptos, that my family may be united at last.'

Setna set sail for Coptos and found the tombs of Ahura and Merab. He ordered their coffins to be lifted and transported in state to Memphis where they were placed beside the coffin of Nefer-ka-Ptah. Then, by order of Pharaoh, the tomb was sealed for ever upon the Book of Thoth.

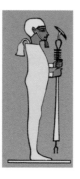

THE LAND OF THE DEAD

There is another tale told of Prince Setna. It is said that his wife bore him daughters but no sons. For many years the couple longed for a boy child, and at last, in their old age, the gods sent them one. Because they believed the child was a reward from the heavens, his parents named him Se-Osiris. This boy was no ordinary being. He was so quick to learn that when he went to school he soon knew everything his masters could teach. He could discuss learned matters with the most respected Wise Men of the House of Life, who marvelled at his knowledge. At twelve years old he was able teach his father many things, for though Setna was a skilled magician Se-Osiris was more skilled by far.

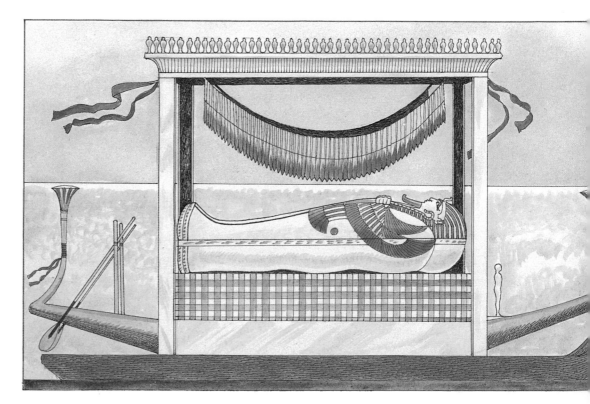

One day, Setna and his young son were walking in Thebes when they heard a sound of wailing and saw a funeral procession making its way through the streets. Servants dressed in fine linen were pulling the funeral sledge towards the river, to set it on the boat that would take the departed one on his last trip across the Nile. On the western bank, where the dead are buried, his splendid tomb would be waiting. For this was plainly the funeral of a rich man. Hired mourners drew everyone's attention with their loud laments. Priests burning incense led the way. Behind came the sledge with its magnificent load – a brightly painted mummy case, embossed with gold and shaped like the mummy within. The likeness of the dead man's face was painted on its lid, and his proud features seemed to approve the pomp and show of his departure. Following behind him came a long file of servants carrying his luggage for the next world – food of all kinds and furniture, linen robes laid in chests, necklaces of gold and turquoise, a hunting chariot and games to play. All these things he required in his tomb, so that he should lack nothing in the Land of the Dead.

After this great procession came the body of a poor man, wrapped in a

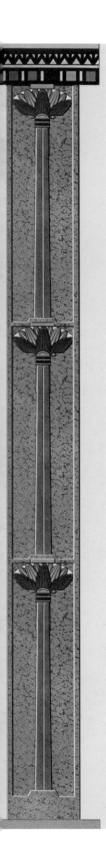

reed mat. His son was dragging it to bury in some pit in the desert sand. There were no followers to weep for him.

'How much happier is the rich man, even in death,' said Setna.

'Do not believe it, Father,' replied Se-Osiris. 'I would not have you treated like the rich man. You will be received in the Land of the Dead exactly as this poor man is.'

'How can you wish that for me?' exclaimed his father.

'Come with me and I will show you,' said Se-Osiris, and taking his father by the hand, he recited words of power. At once the ba-spirits of Setna and Se-Osiris left their bodies, in the form of birds. They spread their wings and flew towards the setting sun just as its light was disappearing over the edge of the desert.

Then Setna, in wonder, saw the sun's boat, the Boat of a Million Years, and within it Ra in his glory, with his attendant gods. And also in the boat he saw the ka-spirits of the dead, all those throughout Egypt who had died that day. The boat passed through the gap in the Western Hills by which it made its nightly journey to the Duat, the Land of the Dead.

'Stay close and follow,' the ka-spirit of Se-Osiris told his father, and their two spirits passed over the horizon and into the night.

The doors of the Duat were flung open and the Sun God entered the first of night's many regions, all of which he had to pass through by dawn. Setna saw a company of gods towing his boat, with golden tow-ropes, along the river that flows through the world of the night, a place of utter darkness. Attendant serpents blew fire from their eyes to light the route and drive away the demons and hideous beasts that lurked on either bank.

'Where are the ka-spirits going, that travel in the boat?' asked Setna.

'To the Judgement Hall of Osiris – you will see!' his son replied.

The boat was now approaching the doors that opened on the second division of the night. Three powers guarded the gate: the Doorkeeper, the Watcher and the Questioner. All who hoped to enter must address these powers by their secret names or perish, and they must name the great gate also by its name. The pilot of the sun's boat spoke these words of power and the boat passed safely through. It crossed the second, third, and fourth

divisions where Ra's enemies lay bound in chains, and came to the fifth gate, the entrance to Amenti, the realm of Osiris. At the words of power the great doors turned upon their pivots, and Setna saw that one of the pivots turned in the right eye of a man that lay beneath it, so that he screamed with the pain of the pivot turning in his eye.

The kas of the newly dead descended from the boat, which went on into the night. 'Where will it journey now?' asked Setna.

'Through the twelve divisions of the night,' said Se-Osiris, 'past the terrible kingdom of Seker where the river runs dry and the boat is drawn through barren sands, and on towards the dawn. Ra travels the waters of the sky by day and the river of the Duat by night. At the sixth division he turns his face to the east and steers his course towards the Mountains of the Sunrise. But Apophis the serpent is waiting to devour him. Every night he fights with Ra, and if Ra fails to overcome him the sun will not rise.'

Then Setna and Se-Osiris entered the Judgement Hall. Its ceiling was of fire and its walls of living serpents. There Osiris, wrapped in the mummy bandages of the dead, presided over the forty-two judges who sat in the Hall of Truth. Isis and Nephthys stood behind his throne. Before him was set a pair of scales. The jackal-headed god Anubis adjusted the scales with care, to see that their balance was perfect, and placed a feather in one of the pans. This was the Feather of Truth, against which each dead person's sins were weighed. Then Anubis took the heart of one of the dead and set it on the other pan. This was the heart of an evil-doer. In desperation, its owner recited the magic formula that he had learned so carefully against this dreaded moment, 'Oh my heart! Do not testify against me. I have not done evil; I have not defrauded any man; I have not done violence to any man; I have not robbed the temples of their offerings; I have not taken milk from the mouths of children; I have destroyed wickedness. I have fed upon truth.'

His words were in vain. The heart was so weighed down with his bad deeds that it tipped the pan lower and lower. Ament, the Devourer of Hearts, who sits for ever by the scales, slavered as he waited for his moment. He had the head of a crocodile, the body of a lion, and the rump of a hippopotamus; each heavy heart was his to eat. He ground between his teeth the heart of this evil-doer, whose spirit was driven into darkness to dwell with Apophis in the pits of fire.

Thoth, the recorder of the gods, stood by the scales and noted every judgement. The next ka that came forward was that of the poor man who had gone to his grave wrapped in only a mat. His heart was set on the pan; again the balance tipped, but it was the heart, this time, that rose high in the air. Then the forty-two judges cried, 'He has not sinned! He has not done evil! The eternal bread of Osiris shall be given to him!' Horus took the poor man's ka by the hand and led him before Osiris, who welcomed him to live in plenty in the Fields of Reeds for ever.

Setna watched all this in wonder. 'And what has become of the rich man?' he then asked.

'It was he whom you saw with the pivot of the door turning in his right eye,' his son replied. 'As he did on earth, so is it done to him. That is the unchangeable law of the gods. You see now, my dear father, why I hoped that you might share the poor man's fate.'

Then the two spirits spread their wings and returned to their bodies. And behold, the procession of the rich man had not yet reached the river bank. Setna could still hear the priests chanting and the paid mourners making their shrieks. He thought of the reception that awaited this man in the Duat, and marvelled at the justice of the gods.

THE DOOMED PRINCE

There was once a pharaoh who had no children, which was a great sadness to him. He prayed daily to the gods for an heir, and at last Ra favoured him and decreed that he should have a son. When the baby was laid in his cradle the Seven Hathors visited him. These were the seven goddesses who predicted the fate of every newborn soul; no one could escape the future they foretold.

They gazed sorrowfully at the little prince and declared that death would come to him before old age, through either a crocodile, a serpent, or a dog.

When the pharaoh heard this, he had a tower of stone built to house his son, furnished with all the luxuries that a royal child should have. This tower stood solitary on the edge of the desert, far from the rough and tumble of city life, and the prince's servants were commanded to keep him always safe within its walls.

The prince spent a lonely boyhood in his tower. One day he climbed to the roof and saw a man leading a dog along the road below. 'What is that creature that follows the man?' he asked.

'That is a greyhound,' a servant said.

'I want a greyhound,' the prince declared.

The servant reported this to the boy's father. 'He could have a tiny puppy,' said Pharaoh, 'so that he does not fret.' So the prince was given a greyhound puppy, which loved him and followed him everywhere.

Time passed and the prince grew to be a man. He was restless in the solitary tower and begged his father to let him go out into the world as other young men did, 'For who knows whether I shall meet my destiny early or late? Let me live while I can, for I am dying within these walls.'

With a heavy heart, the pharaoh let the young prince have his way.

He gave him weapons and a fine horse and accompanied him to the edge of the eastern desert. There the two embraced each other and the father said, 'Now go wherever you please.'

The prince rode into the desert with his faithful dog running behind his horse. He journeyed to the north and to the east until he reached the realms of the King of Mesopotamia. This king had one daughter, who was very beautiful. She lived in a palace perched on the edge of a cliff, and she could be seen each day at her window, gazing down upon the world below. Her father had made it known that any prince who managed to scale the cliff and reach her window might marry her. All the princes of Syria had tried, but the sheer cliff and high window had defeated them all. Now when the Prince of Egypt arrived he declared he meant to try his luck.

'But who are you?' demanded the other princes.

'My father is an Egyptian charioteer,' replied the prince, for he did not wish anyone to know that he was the doomed son of the pharaoh. 'When my mother died he took a new wife who hates me. So I have fled my home.'

The next day the suitors began their climb, and the prince easily reached the window. The princess, who had been leaning from the window as he climbed, had fallen in love with him and greeted him with a kiss. But the king was furious that the runaway son of an Egyptian soldier was to be his new son-in-law. He ordered the young man to be sent packing at once – back where he had come from. The princess sobbed and wailed and declared she would die if she could not have the man she wanted, and in the end her father was forced to give way. And when he saw the prince he had to agree that such a fine a young man was truly fit to marry his daughter.

After their marriage, the prince confessed to his wife that his life was to be ended by a crocodile, a serpent or a dog. 'Then your greyhound must be killed,' said his wife.

'On no account,' said the prince. 'Besides, he would never harm me.'

'Then I must be forever watchful,' said his wife, 'and preserve you from your fate.'

As time passed, the prince longed to return to Egypt and present his bride to his father. So they said farewell to the King of Mesopotamia, and set off with their attendants and baggage across the Syrian desert. Now one night, as they rested on their way, the princess saw a snake gliding towards the truckle bed on which her husband lay asleep. Having a cup of honeyed wine in her hand, she put it in the serpent's path. The snake smelt the sweetness and drank until overcome by the fumes of the wine. When it lay limp, the princess cut off its head. 'See,' she said when her husband woke, 'Ra has given me the first of your dooms, and I will pray to him to give me the others too.'

Great celebrations marked the homecoming of the prince. He took his bride to live in the tower, which no longer seemed like a prison. A garden was made for the princess to wander in, and a park that ran down to the Nile.

Now all this time a crocodile had been waiting in the Nile for the prince's return. But whenever it clambered out of the water to waylay him, one of the marsh giants who lived nearby, who loved the prince, drove it back. One day the prince was hunting in the park and his greyhound chased a gazelle into the Nile. The prince splashed in after them. Then the crocodile

seized him in its jaws. 'Behold I am the doom which ever follows you,' it said. 'By whatever road you go, I shall know how to reach you. But if you will destroy the marsh giant who confines me to these waters I shall this time spare you.'

'Shall I kill one who has protected me!' exclaimed the prince. 'I will not do so.'

So the crocodile dragged the prince under the water and took him to a mud bank to devour him.

But the dog had understood its master's peril. Its frantic barkings brought the princess running. She waded into the reeds and struck the crocodile's snout again and again with a stick. The beast would not release its jaws, but the princess's cries and the lashing of its tail roused the marsh giant from his squelchy bed. He lifted the crocodile and crushed it in his hands.

'Now Ra has given me your second doom,' exclaimed the princess, 'and he will give me the third also.'

All this time, the princes of Syria who had failed to win the princess were burning with anger because she had been given to a runaway and a nobody. They demanded that the King of Mesopotamia should pay each of them the equivalent of her dowry, and when he would not, they warred against him and took him prisoner, saying he must hand his daughter over to them. 'She is not here,' said the king. 'Her husband has taken her I know not where.' So each of the princes led a band of armed men in search of the couple, agreeing that whoever found them should kill the husband and take his wife.

Now those who searched in Egypt soon learned that the pharaoh's son had returned with the Princess of Mesopotamia, and tracked him to his lonely tower. The prince was warned that armed enemies were approaching, and having only a few servants with him, he led his wife to safety in the desert caves. There they hid as the Syrians passed close by, never seeing them. But the dog rushed barking from the cave to defend its owners and a Syrian prince recognized it and turned his men back. The princess threw herself before her husband to protect him but was run through with a spear and fell lifeless. The prince slew many Syrians with his sword and the dog took others by the throat, but enemy numbers overcame them and left them stretched on the ground to be eaten by the jackals. The Syrians marched back rejoicing and divided the lands of the King of Mesopotamia between them.

The dying prince gazed at the bodies of his wife who had tried in vain to save him and his dog who had unwittingly brought about his death. 'O gods,' he cried, 'though I have not offended you, yet I could not escape my fate.'

Thus it was through his faithful dog that the prince at last met his doom. But some say that the gods grieved, and that Ra took pity on the prince and princess and gave them life again.

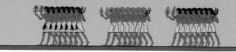

GLOSSARY

Abu The legendary spot which was the first dry land to emerge from the waters of Nu when the world was made. The Ancient Egyptians believed this to be the island of Elephantine in upper Egypt, at the first cataract of the Nile.

Anubis The son of Nephthys and Set. He was the god of embalming and protector of mummies in the tomb. He is represented with the head of a jackal.

Apophis The serpent who was the embodiment of evil and sometimes equated with Set. It continually tried to destroy the sun and throw creation into chaos. At dawn and sunset the sky was red with the blood of Apophis, which was shed in his battle with the Sun God.

ba One of the immortal parts of a human being. The Ancient Egyptians believed each person possessed a body and several distinct spirits. The 'ba' was the imperishable force within a person. It was represented as a bird with the head of its owner and was often shown hovering over the mummy to which it belonged.

Bast A cat-headed goddess who was especially worshipped at Bubastis, a city on the Nile Delta. Cats were sacred to her and lion hunting was forbidden during her festival.

cataract The place where a river bed descends steeply to form rapids or a waterfall. The River Nile has two cataracts.

Duat The Underworld, or Duat, was a place of darkness, yet a source of life. The sun was renewed by its nightly passage through it and Osiris reigned there, giving life to the souls of the just. It was said to contain many sections, with demons, poisonous serpents and lakes of fire.

Geb The god who represented the earth.

goad A spiked stick used for urging cattle forward.

Haroeris Isis is sometimes said to have had four children, sometimes five, the additional one being Haroeris, a form of Horus the elder. Over the centuries myths were often reinterpreted by priests in order to support a particular belief. This gave rise to many inconsistencies. Horus was usually said to be the son of Ra, not of Geb as claimed in the myth of the five extra days.

Hathor The great mother-goddess is shown with the head of a cow, or as a woman with cow's horns. She was the goddess of dance, music and love.

Horus Many conflicting myths cluster around the god Horus. Horus the elder was a hawk-headed sky god. He came to be regarded as the son of Ra and was the god of kingship. Each pharaoh was believed to be an embodiment of this Horus. However, Horus the younger

was the son of Isis and Osiris. Eventually, the myths of the two became intermingled – both forms of Horus are said to have battled with Set.

Isis A much-loved goddess who was often appealed to for protection since she was the saviour of her husband Osiris. She took the form of a bird to search for him, and is often shown spreading her huge protective wings.

ka Another of the spirits dwelling within a person, the ka was the life essence. It was its owner's double, which was born at the same time but continued to live after his or her death.

Khnemu A ram-headed god who was guardian of the source of the Nile. In parts of southern Egypt he was regarded as the creator of the universe.

Khons The moon god, especially worshipped at Thebes where he was said to be the son of the Theban god Amun and his wife Mut.

lapis lazuli A blue semi-precious stone.

Nephthys The wife of Set and sister of Isis. Like Isis she was a protector of the dead and the sisters are often represented together, as mourners, in tombs.

Nu The limitless ocean that existed before the world was made, and encircled the whole of creation after it was formed.

Nut The goddess who represented the heavens and whose children were the stars. She was said to swallow the sun in the evening and give birth to it in the morning.

Osiris The god of resurrection, both of growing things, which spring to life again after the winter, and of human life which is renewed after death. Osiris became the best-loved and most widely worshipped god. He is always represented as a mummy.

pot of fire To have a pot of fire put on one's head appears to have been a type of punishment or torture. To put it on voluntarily, as Setna did, would be to do penance. We still speak of heaping coals of fire on someone's head – meaning making them feel remorseful.

Ptah The local god of Memphis and the god of craftsmanship. He is represented wrapped like a mummy, with a shaven head and tight-fitting cap.

Ra The Sun God of Heliopolis who was closely associated with Horus and, like him, is often shown with a falcon head. The sun was Ra visible in the sky; the sun was also said to be his eye.

Set The lord of the desert. He was a local god of southern Egypt and in certain periods was highly regarded. But as the worship of Osiris gained ground Set became identified with evil. He is shown as unidentifiable animal with pricked ears.

Shu He and his sister-wife Tefnut embodied the forces necessary for life – air and water.

Thoth Originally a moon god, Thoth became the god of knowledge. Described as the heart and tongue of Ra, he was the creative intelligence that brought the universe into being. He was represented both as an ibis, or ibis-headed, and as a baboon.

* Answer to question on page 5: In the story of 'The Doomed Prince', the papyrus breaks off at the point where the prince refuses to bargain with the crocodile (page 59).

INDEX